STUDENT SELF-ASSESSMENT

Student Self-Assessment

A powerful process for helping
students revise their writing

Graham Foster

Pembroke Publishers Limited

To Fern Louise Foster

Acknowledgments

The author wishes to thank the following people for specific advice and contributions to the publication: Pat Barry, Bernice Bast, Sandra Brown, Arlene Christie, Dianne Goldade, Gail Graham, Betty Haney, Larry Hope, Toni Marasco, Judy MacKay, Rosemarie Meyers Walter, Bonnie Nelson, Teresa Raymond, Anne Payne, Deb Weldon, Heather Wheatland, and Peter Willott.

The author is especially grateful to Claudette Miller for her thoughtful editorial advice.

© 1996 Pembroke Publishers Limited
        538 Hood Road
        Markham, Ontario L3R 3K9

Canadian Cataloguing in Publication Data

Foster, Graham
    Student self-assessment: a powerful process for
helping students revise their writing

Includes index.
ISBN 1-55138-077-3

1. English language – Composition and exercises – Study
and teaching (Elementary).   2. English language –
Composition and exercises – Study and teaching (Secondary).
3. Students – and Self-rating of.   I. Title.

LB1576.F68   1996   808'.042'07   C96-931059-5

Editor: Kate Revington
Design: John Zehethofer
Cover Photography: Ajay Photographics
Typesetting: Jay Tee Graphics Ltd.

Printed and bound in Canada on acid-free paper.
10 9 8 7 6 5 4 3 2 1

Contents

1. The Fundamental Importance of Student Self-Assessment of Writing

Self-Assessment as a Revision Strategy

Of all the instructional strategies that teachers may employ to develop student writing ability, which are the most powerful? Phrased another way, which approaches offer the most significant benefit to student writers? With the increased emphasis on writing competence in many subjects, especially Science, Social Studies, and, of course, Language Arts, teachers pose this fundamental question with increasing frequency.

Any answer that fails to emphasize student self-assessment of writing is incomplete. Self-assessment of writing, when it emphasizes revision with specific criteria, becomes a powerful method for the development of students' writing ability in all subjects.

When students assess their writing with specific criteria, they engage in a focused, thoughtful revision process. Through such assessment, students confirm that a specific feature is present and is effective in their writing. They decide whether they must change something to make it clear or correct. They determine when to add and when to delete. They may assess their own writing individually with specific criteria, or they may work with a partner or a small group. Central to student self-assessment of writing is that writers make their *own* final revision decisions; an equally important guideline is that revision criteria be as specifically worded as possible.

A Grade 7 class viewed the film *The Climb*. Following the viewing, students wrote a personal response. Here is one of them.

Often when I'm running in a cross-country competition and, half a kilometre away from the finish line, it is then that I discover just how far I can possibly push myself. This is an example of a physical challenge. A mental challenge for me is an important exam. They can be very intense and give your brain a work out. One of the reasons that I prefer to work on my own than in a group is because of the fact that if I do well on a project I can be proud of it but if I don't do well in a group I wonder "Could I have done better if I was by myself?" I accept new challenges in hiking, swimming, school work, dancing and programs because I have lots of things to be proud of myself with. Accomplishment is the best gift you can ever receive. I learned a lesson on values from this film.

Challenged by the teacher to add at least one new relevant fact or idea and to improve the composition's wording, the student revised the final paragraph. Revisions highlighted:

Often when I'm running in a cross-country competition and, half a kilometre away from the finish line, it is then that I discover how far I can push myself. **I know that if I don't, I'll be disappointed in myself later.** *This is an example of a physical challenge. A mental challenge for me is an important* **school** *exam. They can be very intense and give your brain a work out. One of the reasons that I prefer to work on my* **very** *own rather than in a group is because of the fact that if I do well on a project* **by myself** *I can be proud of it but if I don't do well in a group* **then** *I* **always** *wonder "Could I have done better if* **it** *had been by myself?" I accept new challenges in hiking, swimming, school work, dancing and programs because I have lots of* **reasons** *to be proud of myself. Accomplishment is the best* **reward** *you can ever receive. I* **have** *learned a lesson on values from this film.*

The student's efforts to apply specific revision criteria to a piece of writing have resulted in a second draft that is superior to the first. The idea of disappointment is a useful elaboration. In addition, the substitution of the word "reasons" for "things" and "reward" for "gift" makes the piece much more specific.

While student self-assessment of writing is a powerful writing strategy for many students in many circumstances, it is but one of several strategies that writers may employ to improve their writing. It is particularly useful for student writers — especially when students are learning a new form of writing. Specific revision criteria remind students about critical features of these new forms; in checking for these features in their own writing, students internalize the features and improve their writing.

Teachers must be cautious in introducing self-assessment strategies to students, just as they must be in presenting any writing strategies. A writing strategy is a technique or approach used by some successful writers. However, writing is an art, not a craft. Crafts have predetermined outcomes; arts, such as writing, never fit a mould. Any writing strategy that becomes a universal formula misleads students and misrepresents writing. Certainly writers differ in their writing processes as well as their learning processes. Moreover, writers employ different processes for different pieces of writing. In considering self-assessment strategies, students need to determine the amount of revision a draft requires and the specific criteria that will foster the revision. Students who know *how* to revise with specific criteria are well on their way to deciding *when* it is beneficial to do so.

Therefore, in helping students discover the potential value of applying specific revision criteria, teachers recognize that students must learn to determine the different strategies which work best for them for different compositions. Obviously, students need not apply revision criteria that they have already internalized. Students who are competent in a particular writing form need not rely on checklists that novices in the writing form may find useful.

It is a false orthodoxy to insist that first-draft writing must *always* be revised or *always* revised in the same way. Sometimes, a writer's unrevised first-draft writing is superior to other carefully revised writing. With the guidance of their teacher, student writers often benefit from exploring the amount of revision which will improve a draft as well as specific revision criteria which they may find helpful.

Having considered these cautions, teachers still have good reason to encourage student self-assessment of writing. Professional sources on both reading and writing strategies underline that instruction in strategies benefits average and struggling students more than above-average students. Effective readers and writers automatically and effortlessly tap a range of strategies which work for them. Less successful readers and writers benefit when someone lets them in on the secrets by modelling strategies and encouraging their use. For many students, the adoption of strategies is not automatic and effortless. Few of them will effectively engage in self-assessment of writing without a teacher's guidance.

Encouraging student self-assessment of writing with specific criteria often benefits students who are learning a new writing form. For example, the approach would help secondary students who must write a literary essay or a résumé for the first time. It also often benefits students when they apply criteria related to their personal writing goals, such as using precise vocabulary or mastering points of usage. Finally, the approach benefits students when they are learning a new technique, such as creating interesting leads or making effective transitions or parallel structure. The Grade 7 student's revisions to her writing about *The Climb* illustrate how student writing benefits from revision criteria focused on techniques, in this case, use of specific detail and precise wording.

The Research Foundation

Current professional literature about the development of writing skills deals with topics beyond student self-assessment. Professional sources argue that writers are powerfully assisted by teachers who do the following:

- encourage students to write frequently;
- allow students to use writing to learn content as well as to communicate content knowledge;
- encourage students to engage in personal writing to develop self-understanding;
- allow students to write for genuine purposes and audiences;
- seek opportunities for the celebration and publication of student writing;
- confer frequently with student writers and plan for students to confer with each other about their writing-in-progress;
- see praise of students for their achievements in writing as a fundamental component of instruction and assessment.

While all of these program features are important in the development of writing ability, they lose their potency unless teachers recognize student self-assessment of writing as critical. How many times have teachers lamented the following?: "I encourage journal writing and prewriting. I try to link writing assignments to students' personal experiences. I do my best to help students write for interested readers. I often employ writers' workshop approaches. I offer instruction directly linked to what students are actually writing. Still, many students show such limited improvement in their writing skills!" While student self-assessment of writing may not be a panacea, for many students, it is the most important strategy in the development of their writing skills.

George Hillocks, in his comprehensive review *Research on Written Composition, New Directions in Teaching*, has underlined the fundamental importance of student assessment of writing. Hillocks unrelentingly emphasizes the research support for student self-assessment of writing, particularly student use of specific criteria to revise writing. Two key excerpts from his review, published by the National Council of Teachers of English, follow:

- "As will be seen in the meta-analysis section of this review, students who have been actively involved in the use of criteria and/or questions to judge texts of their own or others, write compositions of significantly higher quality than those who have not." (p. 24)
- "As a group these studies conclude rather clearly that engaging young writers actively in the use of criteria, applied to their own and each others' writing, results not only in more effective writing but in superior first drafts." (p. 160)

Hillocks' advocacy of the use of revision criteria by student writers has significantly influenced the teachers whose students' writing is included in this book. All of the work has been collected from classrooms in the Calgary Catholic School District. For several years, many of the district's language arts teachers have noted the positive benefit of students regularly employing specific criteria to revise their writing. Provincial language arts achievement testing confirms that. Since the advent of achievement testing in Alberta in 1984, the grades 3, 6 and 9 students in the Calgary Catholic School District have always scored far above the provincial average in the writing section of the tests. For example, data released in June 1995 showed that 84.2 per cent of the district's Grade 6 students wrote to an acceptable standard compared to 78.8 per cent for the province. Also, 17.8 per cent of the district's Grade 6 students met the standard of excellence versus 13.7 per cent for the province as a whole. Such scores provide additional support for the power of student self-assessment of writing since most language arts teachers in the Calgary Catholic district emphasize the practice.

Self-Assessment of Writing Across Grades and Subjects

Applying specific criteria for revision works equally well for a Grade 1 student learning that sentences begin with capital letters and end with periods and for a Grade 10 student doing a science report that reflects adoption of the scientific method. Indeed, Hillocks argues that since using specific revision criteria results in improved writing, students should be encouraged to do so in all subjects, not just writing completed in Language Arts.

The two cases that follow powerfully illustrate the benefit of student self-assessment with specific criteria. The first is based on the work of a Grade 3 student; the second, on that of a Grade 9 student. In both cases, the student initially failed to follow the teacher's advice to revise writing by applying specific criteria. The students followed the advice in subsequent assignments.

Case One: About mid-year at a suburban school, some Grade 3 students and their teacher negotiated the following criteria for written fiction reports:

- The report identifies title, author and illustrator.
- The report describes the type of book.
- The report describes the main characters.
- The report describes the setting.
- The report describes the story's major problem.
- The report includes a personal response.
- The report compares the book to other books.
- The report has an illustrated title page that mentions the book title and author.
- The report is neat.
- The report has correct spelling, capital letters and punctuation.

For his first book report, Michael, one of the Grade 3 students, did not revise using specific criteria as he had been asked to do. He submitted the following draft to his teacher:

BOOK REPORT

TITLE: *Deep Trouble.*
AUTHOR: *R.L. Stine*
TYPE: *Chapter Book*

My Book report is about Deep Trouble. It is about some people that where trying to catch a mermaid to research on the mermaid. But some other people were triying to steal it from them to bring it to the Zoo and make some money. They took the mermaid and they put the good people in the mermaids aquarium and pushed the aquarium of the boat and then they got out and got the mermaid back.

As part of class routine, the teacher requires students to complete a self-assessment of their work before she grades it. Michael's self-assessment is remarkably close to his teacher's.

	Student	Teacher		Student	Teacher
Title:	½	(1) 1	Illustration:	2½ (3)	2½
Author:	1	(1) 1	-Title	½	½
Illustrator:	0	(1) 0	-Author	✓	✓
Type:	0	(1) 0	-Picture	✓✓ Your picture is great!	
Main Characters:	0	(1) 0	Neatness:	2 (2)	2
Setting:	0	(1) 0	Conventions:	2 (3)	2
Problem:	3	(3) 3	-Spelling	✓	½
Personal Response:	0	(2) 0	-Capitals	½	½
Other Books:	0	(1) 0	-Punctuation	½	1

For his next book report, Michael remembered to complete his revision homework. The result was an improved composition.

BOOK REPORT

TITLE: *The Werewolf of Feverswamp*
AUTHOR: *R.L. Stine*
ILLUSTRATOR: *No illustrator*
TYPE: *Mystery—Horror*

This book is about a boy named Grady.
His Mom and dad are scientists.
Grady, his sister Emily and parents moved to Florida from Vermont to study swamp deer that they got from South America.

Grady met two new friends named Will and Cassie.
Together they explored the swamp.
They were trying to find out What was Making those terrible howls at night when the moon was full.

It turned out that the howls were coming from Grady's new friend Will
who turned into a warewolf when there was a full moon
    Will attacked Grady and Grady's dog saved his life.
But Will bit Grady,
Grady is the new werewolf of fever Swamp.

    I liked this book because there was a Mystery to Solve.
I Never expected Will to be the Werewolf of Fever Swamp.

    R.L Stine has written very many books. I've read Deep Trouble, The
Werewolf of Fever Swomp, Say cheese and Die, The Haunted Mask
and other books by R.L. Stine.

This time in the assessment exercise, both Michael and his teacher were far more positive about the book review.

	Student	Teacher			Student	Teacher
Title:	1	(1) 1	Illustration:		3 (3)	3
Author:	1	(1) 1	-Title		✓	✓
Illustrator:	1	(1) 1	-Author		✓	✓
Type:	½	(1) ½	-Picture		✓	✓
Main Characters:	1	(1) 1	Neatness:		2 (2)	1
Setting:	1	(1) 1	Conventions:		3 (3)	3
Problem:	3	(3) 3	-Spelling		✓	✓
Personal Response:	2	(2) 2	-Capitals		✓	✓
Other Books:	1	(1) 1	-Punctuation		✓	✓

The teacher wrote the following note: "*Michael, you showed wonderful improvement. Did having the criteria help improve your work?*" Michael wrote back just like this: "*Yes, because I new what to do in it.*"

Case Two: A Grade 9 class trying to refine its skill in writing business letters has worked with selections from these revision criteria.

_____ 1. Without going into detail, my first paragraph builds background for the addressee, e.g., introduces the topic.
____ Yes ____ No

_____ 2. My letter clearly indicates its purpose in the first paragraph. The purpose is to _____

_____

_____ 3. My letter focuses its first paragraph on purpose and the following paragraph(s) on important details related to the purpose. ____ Yes ____ No

_____ 4. My letter clearly indicates the actions that I want the addressee to take. My letter requests the addressee to _____

_____

_____ 5. My letter includes **all** of the critical details related to the purpose and action requested. ____ Yes ____ No

_____ 6. If my letter has been assigned, I have checked that **all** of the critical details in the assignment have been included.
____ Yes ____ No

_____ 7. The letter's language is appropriate to my relationship with the addressee. ____ Yes ____ No

_____ 8. I have included a good-will closing. For example: "Thank you in advance for ..." ____ Yes ____ No

_____ 9. My letter includes a complimentary closing, e.g., "Sincerely," or "Yours truly." ____ Yes ____ No

_____ 10. I have included precise and appropriate information related to my letter's purpose. ____ Yes ____ No

_____ 11. My letter employs transition among its paragraphs by use of transition expressions. ____ Yes ____ No; brief reference to a previous point. ____ Yes ____ No

_____ 12. My sentence lengths are varied. ____ Yes ____ No

_____ 13. I have varied the beginnings of my sentences.
____ Yes ____ No. An effective sentence is _____

_____

_____ 14. My words are specific. Particularly precise words are
_____, _____, and _____.

_____ 15. I have checked for errors in spelling and grammar/usage.
____ Yes ____ No

_____ 16. I have accurately noted the date on my letter.
____ Yes ____ No

_____ 17. My letter follows a standard business letter format.
____ Yes ____ No

_____ 18. My envelope follows a standard business letter format.
_____ Yes _____ No

_____ 19. I use a colon (not a comma) after the salutation (e.g., Dear Mr. Jones:). _____ Yes _____ No

---

11615-11A Avenue
Edmonton, Alberta T2B 1K4
June 1, 1996

Mr. Jones
6700 Meadowlark Rd. N.W.
Edmonton, Alberta T5R 1W3

Mr. Jones:

My name is Jerry Michaels. I'm on the student council for Grant Macewan Junior High. We are providing a assembly and lunch for the volunteers. I would really appreciate for you to come and get recognized for volunteering.

The assembly, followed by lunch, will be held on June 21, 1996. The assembly will start at 11:00 a.m. and will last about 2 hours. We would appreciate that you be at our school around 10:45 a.m. The assembly is in the gym, and the lunch is in the staff room. On the menu is turkey and fixings and for dessert strawberry short cake. We ask that you would please reply to our main office by June 14, 1996.

I hope you will come to be recognized for volunteering for our school.

Yours truly,

Jerry Michaels

Jerry Michaels

For a parallel assignment, written later but dated earlier, Jerry attended more carefully to the revision criteria, thereby improving his letter.

Grant Macewan Junior High School
11615-11A Avenue
Edmonton, AB
T2B 1K4
January 3, 1996

Ms. L. Mulley
System Analyst
Wesjave Engineering Ltd.
#510-752-8 Street North
Spruce Grove, AB
T3C 0R5

Dear Ms. Mulley:

It is my distinguished honour to invite you to be a honorary judge at our Science Fair. The Science Fair is being held by the student council at Grant Macewan Junior High, and is on March 27, 1996 at 7:00 p.m.

Upon your arrival we please ask you to make your way to a gymnasium. We would greatly appreciate if you would be at the school around 6:45 p.m.

You will be judging the top 2 projects from each homeroom for grades 7, 8, and 9. For your greatly appreciated volunteering, we will be serving refreshments after the judging is completed. We ask that you please respond to the office by March 13, 1996.

We would be greatly honoured if you will be able to judge our Science Fair.

Respectfully yours,

Jerry Michaels

Jerry Michaels

Jerry's second effort shows improvement. He adopted the conventional format of a business letter by including "Dear" in the salutation. His opening sentence is more purposeful, his sentences are more varied, and his vocabulary is more precise. Lest anyone surmise that practice alone resulted in the improvement, the teacher reported that Jerry was much more conscientious in working with the specific criteria then.

Taking Ownership of Learning

In their commitment to develop students' ability in the assessment of writing, teachers have posed several related questions:

- What general and specific criteria should students use for assessment of their writing?
- What instruction is effective in improving students' understanding and application of specific criteria?
- How do we develop effective assessment forms and procedures for student writing in all subjects?
- How do we connect student assessment activities to other important aspects of instruction — conferences, marking, and use of computers — in a writing program?
- How does student self-assessment of writing connect to other assessment initiatives, peer-editing, portfolios, and performance assessment among them?

The following chapters deal directly with these questions.

Powerful revision of writing is characterized by several assessment features which will be elaborated upon in this book:

- Students frequently employ specific criteria to revise their own writing and their classmates' writing.
- Students employ revision criteria that are appropriate to the topic, role, purpose, audience and format of their writing.
- Students work with revision criteria phrased in plain language.
- Students employ specific criteria to revise writing in all subjects and grades.
- Students articulate their own revision criteria, including criteria related to their personal writing goals.
- Students learn from the inaccurate application of criteria.
- Students apply criteria to reflect on their writing processes.
- Students engage in instruction about the meaning of specific criteria and how criteria can be applied effectively.

These assessment features have a common theme. The students take ownership of their learning — the major benefit of student self-assessment of writing. Doing this, in turn, yields improved writing.

2. Fostering Student Self-Assessment of Writing

The Importance of Specific Criteria

How do teachers effectively promote student assessment of writing in all subjects and grades? To do so, teachers must answer two fundamental and related questions:

1. **What exactly am I expecting students to demonstrate in the composition?**
2. **How can I help students become increasingly independent in assessing their writing for these important features?**

To be helpful as writing instructors, teachers need to do more than recognize excellent writing — many members of the general public can do that — they must be able to articulate *specific features* of excellence appropriate for a given composition. They will then be able to nurture student writing.

Students should *never* be left to guess about expectations in learning, including those for written composition. Student assessment is most productive when students apply clearly articulated criteria to revise their own writing.

The following example illustrates the benefits of teachers and students working from clearly articulated criteria. Students in a Grade 9 class wrote autobiographies. As part of a thorough revision process, a student in the class identified three possible titles and checked that her introduction focuses the reader while it captures the reader's attention.

Draft Titles: *"What Makes Me Unique"*
    "Why I Stand Out in a Crowd"
    "What Makes Me Different"

Final Choice of Title: *"Sarah's World"*

I've often wondered exactly what makes me different from everyone else and what makes me unique. There are some things that I like that most people like too, such as: skiing, cooking, making things, bike rides, all sports (except basketball), sleeping in, staying up late, listening to loud music and doing things with friends and absolutely loving animals. But what I think makes me unique is that I absolutely love all animals (except insects).

Revisions have been highlighted below:

*I've often wondered, **what exactly** makes me different from everyone else and what makes me unique. There are some things I like that most people like too, such as: skiing, cooking, making **materials**, **bike-riding**, sleeping in, staying up late, listening to music and doing things with **my** friends. **I think that what makes me an individual is that I absolutely love all animals (except insects).***

Sarah's revisions result in improved parallelism in an important sentence and a clever, thoughtfully chosen title. While her other revisions are not as effective, remember Hillocks' point that the benefit of revision with specific criteria is cumulative; subsequent first drafts improve following application of revision criteria. Sarah would probably benefit from self-assessment focused on precise vocabulary since she overuses "things." However, her revisions have already resulted in an overall improvement in her composition. No doubt, precise vocabulary will be the revision focus of another day. Through applying specific criteria, student writers can progress beyond their current achievements toward the meeting of new writing goals.

The teacher's ability to articulate specific revision criteria should not prevent students from taking ownership of their writing. Students should often have opportunities to choose what they will write about and which criteria they will emphasize in revision.

A school's writing program is woefully inadequate when teachers direct the content and criteria of all student writing! Numerous professional sources stress that students improve the content, voice and technique of their writing when they choose purposes and audiences. James Moffett and Betty Jane Wagner effectively make the point: "It is amazing how much so-called writing problems clear up when the student really cares, when he is realistically put into the drama of somebody with something to say to somebody else." However, to complete academic requirements, students must sometimes write for externally set purposes and audiences.

Teachers empower student writers when they help students articulate expectations for writing in familiar language. When students enjoy leeway in their writing assignments, teachers can help students to articulate expectations or goals for the writing which they have chosen to complete. When teachers and students cannot specifically articulate what they value in a composition, students will revise it less effectively and teachers will assess it less effectively.

A student's expertise in applying revision criteria becomes particularly critical in essay examinations in any subject. Students benefit when they anticipate essay-test expectations and related revision criteria. They benefit when they frequently apply these criteria before they complete the test. Hillocks' point about the benefit of self-assessment to subsequent first drafts clearly applies to the fire-drill writing conditions of tests.

The following chart relates student work with assessment criteria to the degree of choice in writing assignments. No matter what the degree of choice, students should always apply specific criteria.

ASSESSMENT CRITERIA RELATED TO DEGREE OF CHOICE IN STUDENT WRITING

Degree of Choice	*Assessment Criteria*
The teacher or institution sets writing requirements.	• With the teacher's guidance, all students in the class identify (or anticipate) and apply appropriate criteria for the set requirements.
	• Individual students identify and apply criteria related to personal writing goals.

Degree of Choice	Assessment Criteria
Students enjoy a measure of choice about writing requirements, but must meet certain set requirements.	• With the teacher's guidance, all students in the class identify (or anticipate) and apply specific criteria for the set requirements.
	• Individual students also identify and apply criteria that are appropriate to their particular compositions and to their personal writing goals.
Individual students enjoy total choice about the purpose, form and content of their composition.	• With the teacher's guidance, individual students identify specific criteria appropriate for the purpose, form and content of their compositions, including their personal writing goals.

The Formatting of Specific Criteria

Let us suppose that a teacher and students have determined that in their work with character study, students should employ concrete adjectives to describe characters. In other words, they will try to do better than "mad," "sad," "bad" and "glad." While these words might be acceptable in some circumstances, students who know words such as "thrilled," "exuberant" and "joyful" can write more precisely. Therefore, students decide to revise their character studies by applying a criterion focused on accurate labelling of character with specific adjectives. The teacher would have several options for formatting this criterion — questions, dichotomous scales, rating scales and criterion frames.

FORMAT FOR CRITERIA	EXAMPLES
Question	• What adjectives do you use to describe the character? What alternatives might be more specific?
Dichotomous Scale	• The adjectives that I use to describe character are accurate and specific. ___ Yes ___ No
Rating Scale	• I use specific adjectives to describe character. OFTEN SOMETIMES SELDOM NEVER _____ _____ _____ _____
Criterion Frame	• The following are the most specific adjectives that I use to describe character: _____, _____, and _____.

Teachers sometimes select a question or a criterion frame format to encourage a more thoughtful level of engagement from students. Many student writers will benefit from writing an answer rather than checking a box. If they are unable to cite an example related to a criterion, they are motivated to revise their writing so that the desirable feature is evident. Many of the examples of student assessment criteria included in this book appear as criterion frames.

When teachers seek to make students aware of their options as writers, they sometimes devise a checklist for self-assessment. They hope to encourage students to consider a possibility that they would not otherwise review. An example, developed by senior high English teachers to focus on organization and transition, follows:

A CHECKLIST FOR STUDENT ASSESSMENT OF WRITING

____ • If I have used a title, I have chosen it
    ____ to point to the main idea
    ____ to symbolize a character or idea
    ____ to foreshadow an event
    ____ to achieve humor or irony
    ____ other _____

____ • My introduction is effective because it
    ____ asks an important question related to my purpose
    ____ tells a brief, interesting story related to my purpose
    ____ states a startling fact or example related to my purpose
    ____ tells about a foolish or incorrect view related to my topic
    ____ presents a dramatic event or conflict, an interesting conversation or a description of setting which features movement or action related to my purpose
    ____ other_____
    _____

____ • Each paragraph connects to the next because I have used
    ____ transition words such as "first," "in addition," "finally"
    ____ *brief* mentioning or reference to previous ideas, or
    ____ repetition of key words and phrases
    ____ other

____ • My conclusion is effective because it
    ____ answers a question posed by the introduction
    ____ warns the reader about something related to the writing
    ____ tells a brief story related to the topic
    ____ uses an effective quotation
    ____ predicts something
    ____ makes a surprising or shocking final point
    ____ other _____

The teachers who developed this form recognized that most of their students would be unlikely to use these organizational features due to a lack of familiarity with them. Thus, they presented examples of these techniques to their students before asking students to work with the revision checklist.

Teachers can usefully follow a similar approach to emphasize important textual features which are unfamiliar to their students. When teachers do so, they are wise to focus on a few critical features for the checklist format. In the above example, teachers chose not to focus on thesis statements, topic sentences and the ordering of ideas.

Using that illustrated checklist, a Grade 9 student effectively employed the technique of refuting an incorrect, foolish view to improve his introduction.

VERSION ONE: *People have different ideas about heroes. My hero is not a hockey star. It's my dad.*

VERSION TWO: *While some people may think that a hero must be a successful business man, or a baseball or hockey star, they are foolish. My personal hero is someone I hold very dear in my heart — my father. While other students may laugh at this choice, my dad has proven himself to be a hero.*

Without the checklist's prompt, he would probably not have found such an effective way to introduce his subject.

Considering the Writing Variables

Developing specific criteria for any final-draft composition begins when students review the following variables in their writing:

Topic: What am I writing about?

Role: From whose point of view am I writing — my own, someone else's? For this writing should I use a personal, familiar voice or should I be detached and objective?

Purpose: What am I trying to achieve in the writing? Do I hope to convince, to entertain, to inform, to describe ...?

Audience: To whom am I writing? Is it a specific individual or group or is it a general audience? What is my relationship to this audience?

Format: What particular writing form or forms are appropriate — editorial, narrative, poem, description ...?

Students and teachers sometimes use the acronym RAFTS to refer to these variables:

R ... Role
A ... Audience
F ... Format
T ... Topic
S ... Strong Verb (purpose)

The following chart illustrates a few of the endless possibilities of writing variables.

TOPIC: WHAT AM I WRITING ABOUT?			
EXAMPLES OF ROLES	EXAMPLES OF PURPOSES	EXAMPLES OF AUDIENCES	EXAMPLES OF FORMAT
Self	Demand	Self	Article
Parent	Narrate	Parents	Journal Entry
Character in Book	Plead	Friends	Business Letter
Detective	Persuade	Pen Pals	Poem
Friend	Remind	Employer	Editorial
Teacher	Support	Politician	Short Story
Historical Figure		Author	Essay

Besides focusing students' writing, reflection on the variables very often helps writers discover ideas that they can use in their compositions. For example, students writing about getting into trouble at school would write a different version of events for the principal or their parents than they would for their friends. What they would write for themselves in their diaries would be different again. In other words, simply by changing the variable of audience, students would discover ideas for their writing. The same holds true for the other variables since writing content varies according to role, purpose and format.

After they consider the variables, teachers and students should be able to identify appropriate criteria, especially since specific forms of writing frequently imply choices from the other variables. For example, an editorial implies the purpose to persuade. A writer would want to identify the topic of the editorial, the target audience and the degree of familiarity or detachment desirable to demonstrate as well.

Students in Grade 12 classes in Alberta must write a literary essay according to a set provincial requirement. They have to take the role of anonymous expert to an unspecified audience; the format is expository, implying that a thesis statement is desirable. In one case, the topic was "Choices and Consequences in *Wuthering Heights*." The students' purpose was to explain the consequences of characters' behavioral choices.

As part of a thorough revision process, one student strove to ensure that the composition contained a focused thesis statement, examples of parallel structure and specific vocabulary. In reviewing the thesis statement criterion, the student made the following change:

ORIGINAL THESIS STATEMENT: *Choice of marriage partners often leads to dire consequences and suffering and pain.*

REVISED THESIS STATEMENT: *A hasty choice of marriage partners often leads to dire consequences.*

Through applying the criterion about including a sentence with parallel structure, the student confirmed that her first draft contained a relevant example: "She was used to a dirty, isolated atmosphere and fell in love with Edgar's money, looks and youth." The sentence remained unchanged in the final draft.

However, an impressive improvement occurred when the student checked to make vocabulary more colorful. She transformed this sentence: "Approaching Nelly for advice on marriage, she says that marrying Heathcliff would 'degrade' her." The revision reads: "A **bewildered** Catherine approaches Nelly for comfort and advice. Well aware of her mistake, she marries Edgar after saying that marrying Heathcliff would 'degrade' her."

The following completed form, which is flexible in nature, illustrates that revision criteria should be appropriate to the writing variables in a given composition. In this example, a Grade 10 student exhibits particular thoughtfulness in the revision of a description. Her focused revision resulted in helpful changes to her composition.

Name: _Mary Fisher_   Date: _May 1.96_   Title: _____

I. PURPOSE, AUDIENCE, FORM:

In the attached piece, my purpose is to _describe a beautiful place_ ____

_____

my audience is ____ _teacher_ _____

the writing form is ____ _description._ _____

II. SPECIFIC CRITERIA:

The following criteria are important to the attached piece of writing.

CRITERION: _A dominant impression is emphasized but not_ _____
stated and every aspect of the description combines to the overall effect.

My Self-Assessment/Revisions: _In my writing, I tried to not tell the reader what it was like, but show the reader the details of it._
Ex: "The salty mist that rose from the flowing stream, mixed with the odor of damp moss and vegetation, created a clean, fresh smell that made noses tingle, and the cool fresh mist gave skin goosebumps and left a slightly moist feeling."
CRITERION: _Imaginative word pictures appeal to the senses._ _____

_____

My Self-Assessment/Revisions: _I changed some of the sentences from ordinary words to more descriptive ones. Ex: "The sand of the pretty water..."_
"The low trickle of the bottle green stream."
CRITERION: _Details are arranged logically._ _____

_____

My Self-Assessment/Revisions: _I arranged my details in a specific order which was I started with the larger things and described the overall place. Then I went on to describe what I heared. I then described what the smells were like (smell) and then went on to describe what I saw (sight). The last thing I described was what I tasted and felt. (taste/touch) I organized my description starting at describing the overall place and then working my way down through the five senses._

Students most effectively employ a form like this to assess each draft of a composition. They come to realize that they are close to a final draft when their writing meets the requirement of each criterion. If it does not, further drafting and revising are required.

Teachers may require students to complete such a self-assessment form before a piece is submitted to them for assessment. Teachers usually evaluate the accuracy and efficiency of students' self-assessment of writing. Specific feedback from teachers becomes warranted when students inappropriately assess their own writing.

In assessing a composition, teachers must decide how much emphasis to place on how well students have completed forms such as the one above. If students are learning about revising with specific criteria or are working to improve their ability to revise with specific criteria, teachers would probably assess students on how well they have completed the form. If students have already learned the technique, teachers would not assess students' completion of the form.

Identifying Specific Criteria

Teachers have access to textual and curriculum resources which should assist them in identifying specific criteria for student self-assessment of writing.

In checking these resources, however, teachers may find that they are not always helpful to students. Not all textbooks identify or suggest specific revision criteria for writing. Since curriculum documents are written for teachers rather than for students, teachers must frequently "translate" specific criteria from jargon to language that students can understand. For example, the criterion "The writer's purpose, whether stated or implied, is clearly established and sustained," an example from an Alberta Education scoring guide for Grade 9 Language Arts, might be translated as follows:

- In my writing I am _____ telling a story ____ explaining ____ arguing or _____ with the purpose of _____

- I have checked that I have not wandered from my purpose, that all parts of my writing directly relate to my purpose. ____ Yes   ____ No

Rather than just presenting assessment criteria to students, teachers usually prefer to involve them in coming up with criteria. Engage students in specifying and selecting criteria for a particular composition as part of classroom practice. You can ask students to generate appropriate criteria for a given writing task, then after discussion and exploration, they can prepare their own criteria lists for use in revision of their writing. For students, the key question in the formulation of assessment criteria is: **What criteria are fundamentally important for my topic, form, role, purpose, and audience?**

To help students to articulate criteria, teachers should draw upon students' reading. For students to write well in any new form, they need to encounter many competent examples of the form. For example, if they are going to write a fantasy, referring to their reading of Roald Dahl's *James and the Giant Peach* should be helpful. In analysing text, students and teachers can usefully explore critical features which give the text its competence and quality. Thus, as part of their reading, students develop criteria for their writing.

Teachers can encourage students to read examples of the kind of writing they are being asked to produce. If students are writing film reviews, for example, they should read several reviews in newspapers and magazines. Ideally, they would read conflicting reviews of the same film. In developing revision criteria for their own reviews, students might note topics that frequently appear in film reviews, such as audience appeal, quality of acting, technical features and emotional impact. Students might note the structure of film reviews — the way they are effectively introduced and concluded and the authoritative voice that characterizes them. These features can easily become revision criteria for students' own reviews.

Helping students "read like writers" allows them to identify questions that relate to their compositions. Questions might be as follows: "How do authors bring characters to life?" "How do authors create interest in the introductions of expository text?" "How do authors create suspense?" "How do authors vary their sentences?" Students use familiar published texts to answer their questions. In doing so, they internalize assessment criteria.

Finally, in classrooms that emphasize self-assessment of writing, students suggest alternatives and improvements to published writing. Why not? Assessment criteria apply to all writing, including that of professional or published authors.

Modelling the Application of Criteria

Students who are not used to applying specific criteria to revise writing frequently benefit when teachers and classmates model effective assessment practice. Using a photocopied or projected text, teachers and peers offer comments and suggestions related to specific questions and criteria. The sample text can be supplied by a student volunteer, an anonymous student from another class or the teacher. When teachers and classmates model the application of specific criteria, students learn the meaning of "criteria" as well as how to apply criteria effectively.

Setting the Number of Criteria per Assignment

How many specific criteria should students identify and apply in a composition? The answer depends upon the age and the skill of the writer. Students should always focus on fundamental criteria which apply to their composition. Ideally, individual students should also identify and apply fundamental criteria related to their personal writing goals. These goals, which individual students have identified for their own writing, are often based upon feedback from classmates and from the teacher.

In many cases, students will determine that five to ten specific revision criteria are appropriate. Sometimes, a class will brainstorm a list of criteria with individual students choosing the ones most likely to provide a challenge. Other times, a teacher will focus students on the five to ten criteria most essential to a composition's purpose, audience, topic and format. For insecure or inexperienced writers, teachers should suggest that fewer criteria be chosen.

The chart on page 26 clearly indicates that student writers in a class do not need to work with identical lists of criteria. What a dreary prospect! Effective writing programs challenge students to identify their own writing goals — even when they must cope with externally set requirements.

A teacher challenged her Grade 12 students to write a personal goals statement to guide the revision of an essay entitled "A Comparison and Contrast of *The Painted Door* and *Celebration*." One student wrote as follows:

In order to improve my writing, I will try to use many details to support and better convey my ideas and arguments. In addition, I will try to concentrate on forming proper sentences because I often write sentences that do not make sense to the reader. Another thing I want to work on is a style of writing that will be unique only to me.

After receiving a fellow student's comments on the essay's first draft, the student wrote:

> *After having my work proof-read by my friend and myself, I can now see the changes I should make. My goal to make my writing more formal or to have sentences which make more sense, was a very good one! I can see that my sentences often do not make sense or are structured in an awkward way. Going back, I can see where changes have to be made. In some instances, I will have to change most of a paragraph.*

This brief excerpt from the student's essay shows how sentences were revised to improve clarity.

> FIRST DRAFT: *Although the basic conflict of man vs. nature is the same in the two stories, in each case the reasons for having to struggle against nature are very different. Mabel from "Celebration" is forced to face the cold when Eric locks her out of the house whereas in "The Painted Door," John has chosen by his free will.*

> REVISED TEXT: *Although the basic conflict of man vs. nature is the same in the two stories, in each case the reasons for having to struggle against nature are very different. Mabel from "Celebration" is forced to face the cold when Eric locks her out of the house**, whereas in "The Painted Door," John **faces nature** by his **own** free will.*

The following chart illustrates a record-keeping system for students to monitor their goals for writing. For younger students, teachers may choose to modify the chart into Can Do and Need to Do lists. With the guidance of their teachers, students should identify goals and apply related revision criteria to subsequent writing.

SELF-ASSESSMENT OF GOALS IN WRITING

Name: _James Chan_

Grade: _9_   Date: _March 26/96_

     From: _September 95_   To: _March 96_

           Date   Date

GOALS ACHIEVED	GOALS STILL TO BE ACHIEVED
— *writing is more detailed*	— *to stay focused on the topic*
— *have better idea on what to write on*	— *improve on wordy/clumsy sentences*
— *paragraphs developed better*	— *improve use of commas*
— *precise vocabulary*	
— *varied sentences*	
— *correct use of semi-colon*	
— *better spelling*	
	In my next assignment, I will try to improve: *1) wordy/clumsy sentences* *2) proper use of commas*

In summary, teachers should encourage students to employ specific revision criteria from two sources:

- the writing variables for the specific composition;
- the individual student's writing goals.

Even when students must meet externally set writing requirements, as they revise their writing, they should always assess how well they are reaching their personal goals.

Assessment Criteria and Writing Conferences

Specific criteria, especially criteria that have been identified and selected by students, offer useful focus in student writing conferences.

When student writers confer about revision with other students, with adults or with the teacher, encourage them to take the leadership role.

Let them identify the criteria they wish to focus on during the conference. In revision conferences, it is sometimes helpful for a student writer to identify and explain the criterion that is most evident in the composition before seeking advice about less effectively achieved criteria.

For the revision of writing to be an enduring, personally significant practice, the writing and revision must be owned by the student writer, not by the teacher. Similarly, the student benefits most when articulating his or her own writing goals rather than adhering to goals the teacher has identified for adoption. Students must learn to think for themselves.

What happens if students are inaccurate in their self-assessment of writing, when they inappropriately apply criteria in revision? Rather than viewing it as a serious problem, recognize inaccurate self-assessment of writing as an opportunity for instruction. A genuine "teachable moment" occurs when teachers observe students inaccurately applying a criterion. Teachers may helpfully focus on the meaning and effective application of the criterion through a brief mini-lesson with a group of students. They can also suggest that students apply the criterion again in a subsequent assignment.

In one instance, an adult student indicated that he had checked to see that his introductory paragraph contained a thesis statement which offered a preview for the reader and which indicated the essay's purpose. He had written:

Each year Zebra Construction matches employee contributions to a charitable organization. As chairperson of the Charities Committee, I am pleased to announce that the Heart Fund has been selected to receive our $5,500.00 contribution.

While the student's purpose is clear, the introduction does not offer a preview.

In an informal conference, the teacher asked the student to point out where the introduction indicated purpose and where it offered a preview. When the student reviewed the purpose, the teacher offered praise, but very quickly the student recognized the lack of a preview for the reader. With the teacher's encouragement, he revised as follows:

*Every year Zebra Construction matches employee contributions to a charitable organization. As chairperson of the Charities Commission, I am pleased to announce that the Heart Fund **will receive** our $5,500* *contribution for its educational programs, its support to patients and its ongoing research.*

The student successfully applied the thesis statement criterion in a subsequent assignment.

Any time an author requests advice from an editing partner, it is the author's prerogative to accept or reject the advice. At their best, writing conferences help students focus on how they have applied specific criteria, not on pleasant chitchat and the avoiding of disagreement. However, writing teachers helpfully remind students to engage thoughtfully in peer-revision and to assess all of the advice they receive about their writing. As students can learn from other mistakes, they can also learn from the mistake of uncritically accepting advice about revisions. Teachers recognize the situation as yet another prime opportunity for direct instruction about peer-editing and about the meaning of specific criteria.

Computer Applications to Student Assessment of Writing

Computer technology can offer writers practical assistance in their revision of writing through application of specific, relevant criteria. Students who are familiar with word processing know that they can easily modify, augment, delete and save text. Beyond word processing, there are commercial programs that offer feedback on many writing features, including spelling, overused words, weak verbs, passive voice, other matters of usage, sentence lengths, and organizational patterns.

Since criteria to revise compositions will vary depending on the topic, role, purpose, audience and format, as well as the writer's own goals, writers should use computer programs that apply criteria without considering writing variables or personal goals cautiously. Furthermore, writers are wise to recognize that computer programs lack the sophistication to offer feedback for many criteria, especially those focused on ideas. They should view computer programs as servant rather than master in the revision of writing.

The most promising computer programs, *Writer's Workbench 5.0* (E.M.O. Computer Products) among them, allow teachers and students to select appropriate criteria as well as to recognize program limitations.

Criteria and the Teacher's Assessment of Writing

Teachers are wise to separate *marking* from *evaluation* in their assessment of student writing. When teachers mark student writing, they emphasize accountability, that is, the competence that students demonstrate in their compositions. On the other hand, when teachers evaluate writing, they emphasize instruction, or the nurturing of student writers.

Effective writing teachers always note achievements and strengths in comments or during conferences. Comments such as the following affirm the student and foster personal goal setting: "Your writing is clearly focused on your purpose; your use of a warning to the reader in your concluding paragraph is very effective. Where could you use transition techniques to help the reader connect your main points?" Typically, effective writing teachers make no more than one or two suggestions for any piece of writing, regardless of its strengths or limitations.

In their marking and evaluating of writing, teachers should emphasize the same criteria used by students in individual or peer assessment. When your assessment disagrees with the student's, value the disagreement as a "teachable moment." When several students demonstrate difficulty in applying a criterion to revise their writing, you may decide to engage the group in a brief lesson which reinterprets the criterion and explores related examples from actual writing. When an individual student faces difficulty in applying a criterion, plan to hold an informal conference.

Teacher feedback to students about successful and unsuccessful revision using specific criteria is critically important for personal goal setting. For example, the difficulty that the adult student had in applying the thesis statement criterion was translated into a personal goal for future pieces of writing.

The following form illustrates how teachers and students should employ identical criteria for assessment of writing, how assessment should celebrate strength and highlight a fundamental goal for learning and further revision. Both students and teacher can use such a form. Peer editors can use it as well. If any disagreement in assessment emerges, members of a classroom writing community should view it as an opportunity for learning.

ASSESSMENT FORM FOR WRITING

Name: *Nicole Phillips*   Date: *April 15/96*

For each criterion listed, students and teachers rate the composition by writing the score and their initials in the appropriate box beside each criterion. Peers who assess the composition should also include their initials with the rating in the appropriate box.

CRITERIA	VERY EVIDENT	SOMEWHAT EVIDENT	NOT EVIDENT
— *clear indication of thesis statement in introduction*	6 5 x √	4 3	2 1 0
— *selection of a particular technique to create interest in introduction*	√ x		
— *clear communication of main idea of each supporting detail (preferably in first sentence)*		√ x	
— *use of transitional sentences/ phrases*		√	x
— *use of specific examples/quotes*		x √	
— *variety in sentence structures*		√ x	
— *use of bright, descriptive vocabulary*	√	x	
— *sense of voice (personal first person I, me, my)*		√ x	
— *use of an interesting technique to conclude*	evident but x ineffective.	√	

form continued

EVALUATION OF STRENGTHS/ GOALS ACHIEVED		SUGGESTIONS FOR LEARNING AND FOR REVISION	
STUDENT	TEACHER	STUDENT	TEACHER
Intro	*- good*	*transitional*	*-manipulate*
Conclusion	*introductory*	*sentences*	*ideas in*
Conventions	*technique*	*length was short*	*supporting*
Supporting	*- clearly*		*details to*
details	*separated*		*communicate*
Quotes	*supporting*		*- need to work on*
	details		*transitions*
	- good use of		*-rewrite topic*
	example		*sentences to*
			combine
			technique and
			personal appeal
			-combine short,
			choppy sentences

In the above example of a student's and teacher's use of a form, the student used an "x" to assess an essay entitled "My Favorite Poem." The teacher employed a "✓" for her assessment. The disagreement about the effectiveness of the conclusion opened up an opportunity for focused instruction during a mini-lesson.

Program Co-ordination Toward Student Assessment of Writing

While individual teachers contribute powerfully to the development of students' writing ability, teachers intensify their influence through collaboration with colleagues. To the extent that teachers nurture writing across subjects and throughout the grades, students will more surely grow as writers. Since students benefit through regular application of revision criteria to their writing, teachers wisely encourage the practice over several years.

When teachers co-ordinate student assessment of writing, both they and their students benefit. Many students require frequent repetition to hone a skill or strategy; however, once they become proficient in applying specific revision criteria and in setting personal writing goals, they can use their developing skills to improve a widening range of writing abilities.

Teachers need not fret that they have neglected criteria in any given year. Through program co-ordination, they can work with the confidence that important criteria will be addressed when need and interest warrant. For example, a student had to meet a certain criterion in Grade 7 before moving on to another in Grade 8. The student correctly noted on his "GOALS ACHIEVED" list that he could compose complete sentences. In Grade 8, he used this sentence strength to focus on varying sentence lengths and beginnings. His goal statements would have been filed at the end of Grade 7 for recovery in the next school year. Teachers can include these statements as part of students' writing folders to pass on information about writing strengths.

To the extent that teachers co-ordinate related matters of managing conferences and responding to student writing, students again will benefit. Teachers should promote student leadership of conferences and student involvement in goal setting within the context of a school's writing program. Similarly, schools nurture student writers when *all* teachers separate marking from evaluation and when *all* teachers offer positive and specific feedback throughout the subject disciplines and throughout the grades.

Individual teachers are wise to encourage attention to program co-ordination as part of a school's professional development program. Many teachers and administrators use parent information nights and publications about their school's curriculum as ways to foster talk about key instructional features, including those of their writing program. Parents should certainly be informed of a school's commitment to student self-assessment of writing.

3. Exploring General Categories of Criteria to Assess Writing

Four Types of Criteria

When students and teachers discuss the features that make a given piece of writing effective, their comments fall under four general categories:

- **writing process strategies**
- **content and organization**
- **semantic and syntactic features**
- **conventional usage**

This chapter explores criteria that fall under these categories. From criteria such as those presented here, student writers must choose specific criteria that are appropriate to their purpose, audience, role and format. In addition to the general categories outlined in this chapter, they need to consider criteria specific to a variety of writing forms and purposes. These are outlined in the next chapter.

This chapter recognizes that students require direct instruction focused on general categories and on related criteria, so it features instructional suggestions.

Writing Process Strategies

Teachers' professional literature contains no shortage of resources focused on a process approach to writing. While frequently cautioning teachers against equating a process approach with an arbitrary formula for writing, professional sources, such as Allan Glatthorn and Jane

Hansen, emphasize strategies employed by successful writers during prewriting, drafting, revising and publishing. They frequently argue that individual students improve their writing when they discover and apply strategies that work well for them. Student assessment focused on writing process is a useful nudge for students to widen their repertoire of strategies.

Students may use the following chart over several writing assignments, even over the entire school year, to reflect on important process criteria. They can employ a number code for each assignment to note use of the designated strategy. The chart's inclusion of the column "MY GOALS AS A WRITER" underlines that students should reflect to set specific goals to improve their writing. For example, the self-admonition not to wander focuses the student on writing with structural clarity. Goal setting challenges students to take a risk with strategies they have not yet tried.

THINKING ABOUT MY WRITING PROCESS

	Record Assignment Number Beside Strategies Used	My Goals as a Writer
PREWRITING		
Drawing/Diagramming	-	A • *Stay on my topic*
Observing	- 2 3	— *don't wander.*
Listening to Reader	-	• *Improve*
Listening to Speaker	-	*paragraphs.*
Brainstorming	- 1 2 3	B • *Provide more detail.*
Reading for Information	-	• *Always have*
Role Playing	-	*complete sentences.*
Interviewing	-	• *Elaborate more.*
Questioning	- 1	C • *Use more colorful*
Sharing in Small Groups	- 3	*words.*
Contributing to Discussion	-	• *Check for clumsy*
Viewing Activities	-	*sentences.*
Writing to Explore	-	
Note-Making	-	
Story Boarding	-	

	Record Assignment Number Beside Strategies Used	My Goals as a Writer
REVISING		
Reading Work Aloud	-	
Listening to Work Read	-	
Conferring with Teacher	- *1* *2* *3*	
Peer-Editing	- *1* *2* *3*	
Individual Revision	- *2* *3*	
Individual Proofreading	-	
SHARING		
Taping of Writing	-	
Displaying of Writing	- *2*	
Reading Final Drafts	-	
Publishing Writing	- *3*	
Dramatized Writing	-	
Putting Writing to Use	-	
Other Sharing	- *1*	

The student who filled in this form later used the listed goals as revision criteria. However, once any student demonstrates a working knowledge of the strategies listed on the checklist, such a process checklist would lose its value.

As that checklist reflects, current approaches to writing instruction, indeed, to language arts instruction, emphasize student work in small groups.

To foster productive group work by students, teachers may use assessment criteria to highlight effective small-group operation. Before initiating small-group work, teachers would be wise to review common-sense advice about effective speaking and listening in a group. For example, you might remind students to review their goals, to focus their discussion on the goals, to invite all members to participate and to conclude group work with a summary of the discussion. After the small-group activity, students can employ assessment criteria to reflect on their personal effectiveness in the activity. The goal is that small-group work becomes increasingly focused and productive.

Many teachers have used a variation of the following form to focus many difficult classes over the years. One appears in the current Alberta Language Arts curriculum guide for Junior High. The Grade 9 student's use of the form illustrates the benefit of repeated use.

SMALL-GROUP WORK STUDENT ASSESSMENT FORM

	Criteria	*My Goals for Small-Group Work*
√	1. I helped the group review its task.	*My goal is to stay on task, and finish the product with the*
___	2. I contributed relevant ideas; I stayed on topic.	*given amount of time*
√	3. I listened carefully to other group members.	
√	4. I was open-minded about different interpretations or understandings.	
___	5. I helped the group stay focused on its task.	
___	6. I contributed to the summary which concluded the group work.	
√	7. I encouraged all members of the group to contribute.	

```
┌────────────────────────────────────────────────────────────────┐
│              SMALL-GROUP WORK STUDENT ASSESSMENT FORM            │
│                                                                  │
│              Criteria                  My Goals for Small-Group Work │
│   √   1. I helped the group review its   My goal is to continue  │
│          task.                           to work as well as I worked │
│       2. I contributed relevant ideas;   with my group on this project. │
│          I stayed on topic.                                      │
│   √   3. I listened carefully to other                           │
│          group members.                                          │
│   √   4. I was open-minded about                                 │
│          different interpretations or                            │
│          understandings.                                         │
│   √   5. I helped the group stay                                 │
│          focused on its task.                                    │
│   √   6. I contributed to the summary                            │
│          which concluded the group                              │
│          work.                                                   │
│   √   7. I encouraged all members of                             │
│          the group to contribute.                               │
└────────────────────────────────────────────────────────────────┘
```

In the case above, students in a Grade 9 class used the form twice within a two-week period. The student whose forms are featured believed she demonstrated more of the desired behaviors in the second small-group activity. In her first use of the form, she focused on staying on task and on time management in her goals statement. In her second use of the form, she identified maintenance of productive group work strategies as her goal. It appears that she has internalized features of productive small-group work. Her teacher has confirmed the student's perceptions through observation of groups as they work.

Content and Organization Criteria

Content and organization criteria remind writers to write purposefully to ensure that what they write is focused on their topic and that they provide enough detail. If originality is appropriate for the writer's purpose and audience, these criteria should challenge students to write and structure their writing in an interesting way; content and organization criteria remind students to connect the various parts of their writing and to open and close their piece effectively.

In addition, teachers can craft content and organization criteria to focus students on sense of audience and on voice in writing. Doing this is important because effective writing anticipates a reader's needs in content and structure. Through promoting honesty and originality of content and expression, teachers can allow students to develop writing that is strong in voice, that is, writing for which only the author could have chosen the specific details in the piece and for which only the author could have chosen the specific images and expressions.

COMMON CONTENT AND ORGANIZATION CRITERIA

- The purpose of my writing is to ...
- I have checked that all parts of my writing relate directly to my purpose. ___ Yes ___ No
- I have checked that all of my main ideas are supported with examples, reasons, facts, illustrations or details. ___ Yes ___ No
- The paragraph or section that has the most complete and purposeful details begins with the sentence: ...
- The most imaginative or unusual section related to my purpose is ...
- The part of my writing which best demonstrates that I care about my purpose and topic is ...
- My opening creates interest by ...
- The writing closes effectively by ...
- I effectively employ transitions in the following places: ...
- The main points or sections of my writing have been arranged in the following order: ...
- I have checked that the order of my main points or sections is clear for my reader. ___ Yes ___ No
- The part of my writing that best conveys the sense that no other writer could have written it is ...
- I have checked that my writing follows expectations for its form (e.g., business letter, short story, résumé). ___ Yes ___ No
-

Specific wording and formatting of these criteria must reflect relevant writing variables. For example, appropriate content and organization criteria for stories differ from appropriate content and organization criteria for plays. A criterion for stories might be as follows: "I have written the story from a consistent point of view." This criterion does not apply to plays, where more than one character speaks. A criterion for a play might be: "I have placed stage directions in italics." This criterion is irrelevant to stories.

In addition to helping students work with specific criteria to revise writing, teachers may choose to focus instruction on important elements of writing. Having students show something rather than tell about it is an example. The following instructional strategies should help them improve the content and organization of their writing as well as to become increasingly skillful in applying criteria. Many students will require instruction in aspects of content and organization before they can successfully employ related revision criteria.

1. RAFTS

Purpose: To help students to review critical variables in any writing task and to realize that considering the variables assists writers in discovering ideas.

Review of RAFTS variables helps students to focus their writing. It also helps students discover ideas.

R ... ROLE
A ... AUDIENCE
F ... FORMAT
T ... TOPIC
S ... STRONG VERB (PURPOSE)

Sometimes RAFTS variables are assigned. Whether or not variables are assigned, students should review them as part of prewriting. Stress the idea that the variables are interactive, that is, the role, audience, and topic often limit choices of format.

Example: R ... ROLE ... Concerned citizen
A ... AUDIENCE ... Mayor
F ... FORMAT ... Business letter
T ... TOPIC ... Noise from rock concerts
S ... STRONG VERB ... To complain

2. H-W5

Purpose: To assist students to generate ideas for writing by posing questions used by journalists.

Encourage students to answer and note H-W5 questions about their topic.

H ... HOW?
W ... WHO?
W ... WHAT?
W ... WHERE?
W ... WHEN?
W ... WHY?

3. Graphic Representations

Purpose: To encourage students to employ graphic representations as a powerful prewriting tool to benefit content and organization.

Encourage students to complete a key visual (e.g., thought web) related to the purpose, audience and form of a specific piece of writing.

Examples: The character map, completed by an English as a Second Language student, and the semantic map, completed by a Grade 7 student, improved the content and organization of the students' compositions.

CHARACTER MAP

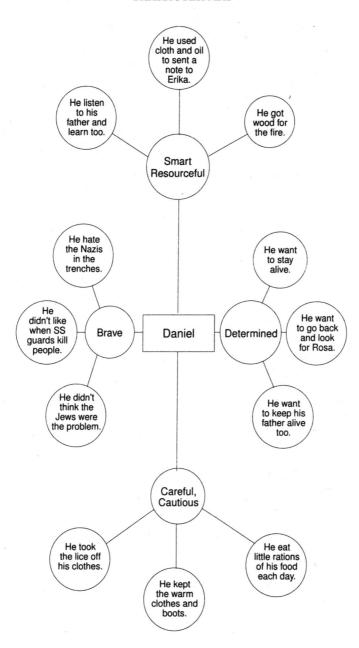

Book: Daniel's Story

THESIS: "IT IS IMPORTANT TO MAINTAIN GOOD HEALTH"
SEMANTIC MAPPING

How to maintain Good Health
Excercise more: sports,
jogging, basketball etc.,
walking and playing
outdoors.
Eat more healthy foods:
foods with less fat, limit
yourself on going to
fast food restaurants
like: Mcdonalds, KFC etc.
Sleep more: Children: 9 hours,
Babies: 12 hours, Adults: 6
hours.
Get vaccinations and have
regular checkups.

If you don't take care of your Health
Smoke: Lung disease,
trouble breathing.
Drugs: Addicted, hurts
your brain, give pain to
your body.
Don't eat well: Eat fat:
heart disease.
Don't eat right amount of
vitamins and minerals: Sick.

HEALTH

Other types of Health
Mental: Being optimistic, having
high self-esteem, playing
and doing things with
friends, laughing.

If you take care of your Health
Have more energy, do things
feel great, be more active,
enjoy life, don't have to be sick
or get viruses and diseases,
longer life.

4. Voice in Writing: Reading Like a Writer

Purpose: To have students use literature that has a strong voice to develop a strong voice in their own writing.

a. Choose a literary work or piece of student writing that is strong in voice. The novels *Angel Square* by Brian Doyle and *Ellen Foster* by Kaye Gibbons are two possibilities.

b. After reading, engage students in discussion about how the voice is distinctive and whether the voice makes the writing effective. Throughout the discussion, list features that create voice in writing on the blackboard or on chart paper. For example:

- honest, personal expression;
- the sound of how people speak;
- insight into the personality of the writer;
- unique expression.

c. Challenge students to compose or to revise a piece to emphasize voice. In revision activities, ask students to identify precisely where the piece is honest, personal and unique in expression.

5. Observational Activity

Purpose: To encourage students to look to their own experiences to generate content for writing.

As a prewriting activity, possibly related to descriptive writing, have students directly observe a scene (e.g., the lunchroom), determine the mood they wish to convey in their writing and select those details they observe in the scene which best create the mood. Challenge students to note details the casual observer might miss. Details might be smells, sounds, and textures, as well as sights. Students should draw on all their senses.

6. Showing, Not Telling

Purpose: To encourage students to show rather than to tell in their writing.

Highlight passages in literature that *show* rather than *tell*.
Ask students to locate sections in their own writing which could be enhanced through showing, not telling. Challenge them to rework the sections. For example, "Mom was angry" could become "Mom stormed into the room, grabbed the telephone off the shelf and slammed it into the wall."

7. Oral Rehearsals

Purpose: To encourage students to employ informal talk often and role playing to generate ideas for writing.

Students benefit from an oral rehearsal or role play before they write. Ask students to tell someone what they want to say; the listener asks questions and seeks to clarify information. More formally, students can effectively role-play about a topic as a net for ideas to write about.

8. Response to Literature

Purpose: To encourage students to use literature to discover ideas for their own writing.

Literature offers rich inspiration for writers' own writing.

Possibilities that sometimes apply to specific literary texts include the following:

- writing about a character similar to that read about in literature;
- writing about a setting which has powerful significance for the writer (possibly inspired by a literary setting);
- writing about an experience similar to that described in literature;
- writing a revised ending or a sequel to a piece of literature;
- writing in the voice of a character in literature;
- limiting the pattern of a literary work.

9. Checks and Stars

Purpose: To allow writers to guide editing partners in improving the content of a piece of writing.

Have student writers place a star beside every paragraph that they believe is clear and detailed. Have them place a check by paragraphs with which they would like help from an editing partner. The exercise focuses the editing partner on the writer's agenda in the discussion that follows.

10. Outlines in Reverse

Purpose: To encourage students to employ outlines after they draft to improve the logic and flow of their writing.

Rather than having students complete outlines *before* they write, have them complete them *after* they write. The exercise should focus students on the organization of their writing:

- Are separate ideas developed in separate sections?
- Do any sections require expansion?
- Should sections be combined?
- Does the writing have an introduction and a conclusion?

Semantic and Syntactic Criteria

Semantic criteria remind writers to choose their words purposefully. Writers should select words and expressions that are appropriate to their audience and form. While writers should almost always strive to be specific and accurate in word choice, they should often try to be colorful and unique, too. For example, technical and scientific writing should be specific and accurate. While narrative and poetic forms should also employ specific and accurate language, the word connotations in these forms add color and uniqueness. The following excerpt from a student's composition illustrates effective vocabulary in a narrative.

> She stood on the steps outside the cathedral. A tiny breeze brushed by, playfully tugging at her hair and clothes. Dried leaves snapped and crackled as they blew past, hovering above her head.

Syntactic criteria are closely related to semantic criteria. They cover varying the length and design of sentences; however, writers must realize that there are exceptions to the rule. For example, a string of short sentences would suggest speedy action. Similarly, although writing complete sentences is usually a good idea for students, literature offers numerous examples of sentence fragments that work well in context. What writers should always bear in mind is that sentence structure should assist the reader in understanding the purpose and content of the piece.

COMMON SEMANTIC AND SYNTACTIC CRITERIA

- I have checked that all of my words are precise. ____ Yes ____ No
- Three particularly precise words are _____, _____, and _____.
- A particularly effective or colorful expression is ...
- I have varied my sentence lengths and beginnings. ____ Yes ____ No
- An effective longer sentence is ...
- An effective short sentence is ...
- I have checked that all of my sentences are complete. ____ Yes ____ No
- I have checked that sentences are correctly ended with a period, question mark, exclamation point, or with a semi-colon between two connected, complete thoughts. ____ Yes ____ No
-

The following instructional suggestions should help students improve the semantic and syntactic features of their writing and to become increasingly skillful in applying related criteria.

1. To Be or Not to Be

Purpose: To encourage students to employ specific, colorful vocabulary appropriate to purpose and audience.

Have students rewrite a section of composition replacing all forms of the verb "to be," for example, "am," "is," "are," "was," "were," and "will be," with an alternative.

Examples: "Sunlight spread across the city."
NOT: "It was a sunny day."

"Clara, the protagonist of the story, faces an identity crisis."
NOT: "Clara is the protagonist of the story."

You can also encourage students to explore alternatives for all forms of "to have," "to go," or "to get."

2. Tired Old Words

Purpose: To encourage students to employ specific, colorful vocabulary appropriate to purpose and audience.

Ask students to identify and underline the three most tired words in a piece of their own writing (e.g., good, bad, excellent, great, mad, sad).

Students should then insert alternatives for the tired words, alternatives that are appropriate for purpose and audience. If students use a thesaurus, they should verify their word choice with a partner.

3. Banned Letters

Purpose: To encourage students to employ specific, colorful vocabulary appropriate to purpose and audience.

For a section of a piece of writing, perhaps one paragraph or a page, ask students to underline all words that contain a letter of the alphabet which you preselect. The letter should be a consonant, such as *c, l, p* or *d.* (Never ban *n* or *s.*) The assignment requires students to insert alternatives for words that contain the banned letter. The exercise should result in increased precision in vocabulary.

4. Word Connotations

Purpose: To encourage students to recognize and to compose connotative language that is appropriate to purpose and audience.

Provide travel brochures or catalogues. Ask students to identify the messages in the brochures — both the explicit and the implicit.

Focus students on the effectiveness of specific words in conveying the message. Introduce word denotations and connotations. Word denotations are the literal meanings of the words; word connotations are the implicit or suggested meanings. Ask students to describe the connotations of selected words from the travel brochures.

Once they have read the brochures, challenge students to create their own with specific attention to word connotations OR have students revise a piece of writing to improve the connotations of selected words.

5. Choice Words

Purpose: To encourage students to recognize and to compose colorful language which is appropriate to purpose and audience.

As part of the reading of a work of literature memorable for its precise vocabulary, challenge students to note choice words (**not** phrases) and to relate these words to the author's meaning. Beryl Markham's *West with the Night* and John Knowles' *A Separate Peace* are prose works characterized by connotative vocabulary. If students are capable of learning the meaning of connotations (implied meaning), the understanding should enhance their sense about why words are "choice."

Challenge students to move from the reading of literature to the reading of their own writing and to revise at least three words (**not** phrases) so that these words, too, can be labelled as "choice."

6. Choice Imagery

Purpose: To encourage students to recognize and to compose effective imagery which is appropriate to purpose and audience.

55

As part of the reading of a work of literature memorable for its original imagery (appeal to the senses), challenge students to note choice images (**not** words) and to relate these choice images to the author's meaning. Many of the images will be figurative (metaphors, similes, personifications); while labelling may be helpful, the major emphasis should be placed on the effectiveness of the images.

Challenge students to move from the reading of literature to the reading of their own writing and to consider whether choice imagery would be helpful (it isn't in some writing). Students should each choose a piece of writing which can be revised to include at least one choice image.

7. Creative Cloze

Purpose: To encourage students to employ specific, colorful vo-cabulary that is appropriate to purpose and audience.

Choose a brief reading for your class related to work-in-progress. Leave out a few selected words, words with powerful connotations. Poems and students' writing samples, used with permission, work well in this activity. Individually or in small groups, students select words that fit. Next, they compare their versions with the original. Finally, students determine whether any of their word insertions are more appropriate, specific or creative than the original word choices.

8. Reverse Psychology

Purpose: To encourage students to employ specific, colorful vo-cabulary that is appropriate to purpose and audience.

Challenge students to *ruin* a brief passage which has precise vocabu-lary by rewriting the passage in dull, ordinary language. Or, you could present students with a dull version first (possibly re-created by other students in response to the precisely worded version) before they read the precisely worded version.

9. Character Charts

Purpose: To encourage students to employ specific vocabulary to describe characters.

Challenge students to create pie charts for plays, novels and stories they have read. The chart should contain one clue and at least four words to identify the character.

Example:

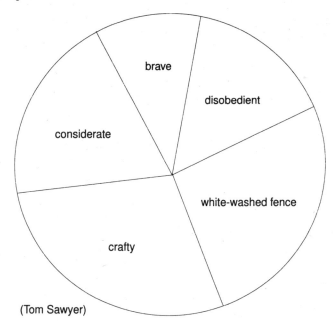

brave

disobedient

considerate

white-washed fence

crafty

(Tom Sawyer)

10. Sentence Expansion

Purpose: To encourage students to employ varied sentence patterns to show the relationship between ideas and to add interest for the reader.

Choose a brief text written by a student or published author. Reduce the text to simple sentences. Present the simple sentences to the class as a handout or as an overhead transparency. Challenge students to combine the sentences to connect the ideas and to show how the ideas are related. Work with students to compare their versions with the original to determine which patterns work best. Keep an open mind! Sometimes, students' versions are better than the originals. Finally, challenge students to revise a piece of their own writing to achieve sentence variety.

11. Sentence Options

Purpose: To encourage students to employ varied sentence patterns to show the relationship between ideas and to add interest for the reader.

Remind students that sentence patterns show the relationship among ideas.

Example: I was late for supper **and** it was cold when I ate it.

And suggests that the two ideas are of equal importance.
To show the relationship between the ideas, another sentence pattern is preferable.

Since I was late for supper, it was cold when I ate it.

or

Arriving late for supper, I had to eat cold food.

Encourage students to focus on the sentence patterns in literature that they are reading; they will note the connections between patterns and meaning.
Ask students to each rewrite a section of one of their compositions so that they more clearly demonstrate how ideas are connected.

12. Periodic Sentences

Purpose: To encourage students to employ periodic sentences effectively when they wish to create suspense or to build to a critical point.

Most sentences begin with the subject (what the writer or speaker is discussing) and then say something about the subject — what the subject is or does. These are called loose sentences.

Example: The thief crept into the dark, silent study.

To create interest and suspense, writers sometimes use periodic sentences which delay the subject and predicate.

Example: Into the dark, silent study crept the thief.

Overused, periodic sentences lose their impact.

Challenge students to find a periodic sentence in literature and to judge its effectiveness. They can then transform one of their own sentences in a piece of writing. Once again, students should judge its effectiveness.

13. Active and Passive Voice

Purpose: To encourage students to consider transformation of sentences from passive to active voice.

If you find that passive voice is overused in students' writing, teach about active and passive voice, stressing that the active voice is usually preferable.

Active voice construction is more direct and less awkward. In passive voice construction, the subject is the receiver of the action.

Examples:

PASSIVE VOICE	ACTIVE VOICE
• The prize was received by many.	• Many received the prize.
• The villain was foiled by Sherlock Holmes.	• Sherlock Holmes foiled the villain.
• The Internet was used by the president to proclaim his message.	• The president proclaimed his message on the Internet.

Encourage students to identify examples of passive voice in their writing and to recast sentences in the active voice.

14. From Observation to Varied Sentences

Purpose: To encourage students to employ varied sentences to indicate the relationship among events.

Ask students to use a notepad to record, in point form, observations about what happened at a school event such as a pep rally. Later, challenge students as a whole class to combine the points into sentences to show relationships.

Example: - at pep rally, Mary pushed pie into principal's face
- principal screamed and jumped
- principal chased Mary out of the gymnasium

After Mary shoved the pie into the principal's face at the pep rally, the principal screamed, jumped and chased her around the gymnasium.

Conventional Usage Criteria

Just as they identify other criteria, students and teachers should select conventional usage criteria that relate to a composition's writing variables. For instance, business letters demand formulating and punctuation related to the form; on the other hand, sentence fragments may be appropriate in stream-of-consciousness writing or diary entries. Since they are constantly bombarded by advertising, students know that unconventional usage can be effective and profitable. Still, teachers are remiss if they do not remind students that conventional usage, including spelling, punctuation and grammar, is usually appropriate and necessary. Student writers must learn that conventional usage is a code that enhances clear communication between writer and reader.

Teachers are wise to take a diagnostic approach when it comes to identifying what conventional usage criteria students should work with. The criteria can highlight usage problems that students are struggling with in their writing. For example, if a Grade 2 student often forgets that the first word of a sentence begins with a capital letter, that can be translated into a criterion for future writing.

Teachers should encourage students to take responsibility for overcoming usage problems. Promoting the use of handbooks and reference books is desirable. They can also remind students to check their writing for Personal Usage Demons. For example, anyone who is prone to drafting sentence fragments should check each sentence with a complete-sentence criterion in mind. In proofreading for Personal Usage Demons, students will learn that they should not underestimate the value of using specific criteria.

What often works well is for teachers and students to negotiate criteria that are important for all students in the assignment first. As previously mentioned, it is always a good idea for students to generate their own criteria and to work with criteria phrased in familiar language. In addition to working with these shared criteria, individual students can identify three or four criteria that are personally important to them. Very often, these criteria will be matters of conventional usage.

The following instructional suggestions should help students master conventional usage and to become increasingly skillful in applying related criteria.

1. Spelling Demons

Purpose: To encourage students to identify and to correct spelling errors from their own writing.

Regularly (possibly weekly) encourage students to generate a list of their five worst Spelling Demons. Also, review specific spelling strategies with the class. You might want to refer to Ruth Scott's *The Student Editor's Guide to Words* (Gage), a valuable handbook on spelling rules and strategies. Ask students to use such strategies to help them learn and remember the correct spelling of their personal word demons. Have students test each other on personal spelling demon words often. More importantly, require students to edit their own writing for Spelling Demons.

2. Dictation Exercises

Purpose: To encourage students to use dictation to learn about conventional usage.

a. As a brief exercise, at normal speed, read the class a paragraph related to work-in-progress (e.g., from a current story or textbook reading).
b. Read the selection again in short phrases so that students can copy the words. Do not repeat anything.
c. Read the passage again at normal speed so that students may proofread their work.
d. Next, ask students to look at the passage read and circle the errors in their own versions. Student partners should then check to note errors that students did not circle.

Remember that the brief exercise is designed to focus on *learning about* conventional usage rather than on *demonstrating* knowledge. Foreign language teachers use it frequently.

3. Conventional Usage Centre

Purpose: To encourage editing of students' writing through use of reference material.

Establish an area of the classroom for reference handbooks and collections of exercises focused on frequent usage problems.

During revision, encourage students to use handbooks. After conferences or assessments, ask them to employ handbooks and exercises to revise one or two usage errors in their own writing. *Language Arts Survival Guide* by Margaret Iveson and Samuel Robinson (Prentice-Hall) and *Language to Go* by James Barry (Nelson) are two useful student handbooks.

4. Exercises in Mechanical Proofreading

Purpose: To encourage students to apply specific proofreading strategies to improve mechanical aspects of their writing.

Encourage students to adopt the following narrow-focus strategies:
  a. running a blank sheet of paper slowly down a composition so that they must read one line at a time;
  b. reading one sentence at a time from the bottom up to take each sentence out of context and thus focus on mechanical errors, not meaning;
  c. circling all suspected spelling errors before consulting a dictionary;
  d. reading the piece aloud to themselves or a friend, or reading into a tape recorder and playing it back;
  e. listing three of their most frequent errors at the top of the paper, then reading the paper three times, each time focusing on one of these errors.

Challenge students to apply these strategies to their own writing.

5. Goal Setting for Usage

Purpose: To encourage students to correct errors in conventional usage in their writing.

Have students keep a section of their notebooks or three-ring binders entitled "CONVENTIONAL USAGE." In the section, students can file work that they have done to meet the challenges to conventional usage which emerge from their own writing. The first page of the Conventional Usage section should list goals achieved and goals still to be achieved.

The Value of Supportive Instructional Strategies

While the instructional strategies described in this chapter should be appropriate in any writing program, they are particularly powerful in programs that emphasize student self-assessment of writing. Through the instructional strategies, students learn about what the criteria mean. They need to know this in order to apply criteria successfully.

4. Identifying Criteria for Selected Forms and Purposes

The Importance of Selectivity

This chapter offers suggested criteria for a variety of purposes and writing forms. Teachers and students should select criteria carefully since no revision criterion is universally applicable. They should determine appropriate criteria by considering writing variables and personal writing goals. Advice presented in writing textbooks and handbooks will aid students in developing criteria for various purposes and writing forms.

Learning Logs and Personal Responses to Literature

Learning logs and written personal responses to literature are examples of writing to assist students' learning. Their use can foster risk taking, develop understanding and consolidate learning. Therefore, it makes sense for teachers to employ student self-assessment to nudge students towards making more detailed, varied and thoughtful responses.

One Grade 8 science student, typical of many, used a learning log to summarize with a minimum of detail. Then, through use of criteria from a self-assessment checklist four times during a school term, he expanded his range of thinking. He included questions, comments and proof of his developing understanding. His responses increased in both length and thoughtfulness.

As students complete learning log entries and written personal responses to literature, the teacher functions, ideally, as trusted adult rather than judge. Marking students when they write to learn would be counterproductive. Teachers, instead, should view writing to learn as a way for students to improve their writing to communicate. When students can articulate what they need to learn, it helps teachers focus instruction.

The following list of common criteria provides several options for student writers to consider. Such a list would not be adopted whole, but seen as a resource.

LEARNING LOGS/PERSONAL RESPONSES TO LITERATURE: COMMON CRITERIA

- My entries reflect various types of thoughts: ___ comments; ___ questions; ___ predictions; ___ likes/dislikes; ___ personal connections/examples; ___ judgments; ___ arguments; ___ descriptions; ___ illustrations; ___ observations; ___ doubts; ___ developing understandings; ___ evidence of changing my mind; other _____
- My entries are thoughtfully completed and detailed. ___ Yes ___ No. My most thoughtful entry is ...
- My entries summarize what I have learned. ___ Yes ___ No. My most effective summary of learning is ...
- My entries reveal when I am unsure about something. The best example of when I deal with uncertainty is ...
- My entries include goals. An example is ...
- My entries show honesty. My most honest response, the one in which I reveal opinions, feelings and doubts, is ...
- My entries sometimes comment on the views of others as well as on my personal experiences. An example is ...
- My voice as a writer, my own way of saying things, is evident. It is clearest in the following entry: ...
- My entries pay attention to important features in my reading, for example, choice of language, author's voice. The best example is ...
- My entries reveal what I enjoy in reading. The response that best illustrates this is ...
-

Description

Although description is usually blended with another writing form, students often write descriptions in school. This type of writing purports to create a dominant impression or emotion through carefully selected details. Imagery and vocabulary matter greatly. Teachers might usefully remind students that effective description usually expresses an idea implicitly rather than explicitly. For example, instead of stating that the room was messy, writers should convey messiness through concrete words describing the scene. "The floor was strewn with pieces of red and yellow Lego, obviously caught in an earthquake, a score of plastic knights and half a dozen Brio train wrecks." A focus on descriptive writing helps students to learn how to "show" rather than "tell."

One Grade 10 student discovered that by combining criteria from a self-assessment checklist with direct observation she improved the quality of her descriptive writing. By adopting the writing process criterion of observation, she sharpened the detail and emotional impact of her description of the school cafeteria at lunchtime. She was better able to meet description criteria related to imagery and unique detail.

DESCRIPTION: COMMON CRITERIA

My writing conveys a single dominant impression. ___ Yes ___ No. The dominant impression conveyed by my description is ...

- I have checked that I have suggested but not directly stated the dominant impression. ___ Yes ___ No
- The details that most effectively suggest the dominant impression are _____, _____, and _____.
- By placing details in the order I have selected, I am emphasizing ...
- The most unusual detail is ...
- My most imaginative images (word pictures) are _____, _____, and _____.
- My most colorful words are _____, _____, and _____.
-

Poetry

Teachers often surprise students when they say that poetry requires at least as much revision as any other form of writing. Students often assume that because poetry expresses intense emotion and thought, suggested revisions are an attack on the author! Of course, anyone entrusted with response to someone's poetry should be discreet and positive; editors should always offer suggestions in the spirit of improving the expression of emotion and thought, rather than in criticizing it. With its concentration of language, poetry challenges student writers. Appropriately selected self-assessment criteria assist students to become more confident with the form. The following criteria apply best to lyric poetry, not to narrative or dramatic poetry.

A Grade 11 student reported that, as a result of using a checklist including some of the above criteria, he questioned how poets write endings for their poems. He read several examples and observed that many poems conclude with an unusual twist or with emphasis on a final point. This insight assisted him both in reading and in composing and revising his own poetry.

Narration

Character, setting, plot, and theme are essential ingredients in stories. However, since stories vary in their emphasis on these elements and on other elements, such as point of view, irony, and symbolism, students should apply only those narrative writing criteria that relate to the writing variables of topic, role, purpose, audience, and format.

One Grade 11 student who enjoyed writing stories so much that he did so voluntarily was dissatisfied with his ability to compose. When he completed self-assessments, he appreciated that his writing possessed many desirable features. However, the exercise motivated him to "read like a writer." After reading several examples of effectively focused stories characterized by realistic dialogue, the student became freer from adding irrelevant details and drafting somewhat stilted dialogue.

NARRATION: COMMON CRITERIA

- Characters are lifelike; their speech is realistic and individualistic. ___ Yes ___ No. My most lifelike character is _____ because ...
- The best illustration of character motivation, that is, reason for behavior, in my narrative is ...
- The protagonist changes as a result of the events in my story in that he/she ...
- The author's point of view (person who tells the story) is _____ because ...
- The section of the plot which best shows action and character rather than just telling about them is ...
- My story's conflict is ...
- My story focuses on the thoughts and feelings associated with conflict when it ...
- The climax to my story is logical because ...
- I have checked that every event in the story clearly connects to every other event, to the conflict and to the climax. ___ Yes ___ No
- My story's most lifelike dialogue is ...
- Emphasized details of setting are ...
- My story suggests the following insight or theme: ...
- My story's title has been chosen to ...
- I have thoughtfully used several techniques: ___ flashback; ___ irony; ___ symbolism; ___ other _____
- My reason(s) for using the technique is (are) to ...
-

Friendly Letters

Although people are writing fewer friendly letters and making more long-distance telephone calls than they did a generation ago, students can enrich their lives through well-written friendly letters. Also, many write them at school, especially in Grades 4 to 7. Friendly letters offer elaboration about one's life usually uncharacteristic of telephone calls. One Grade 7 student moved beyond a "bed-to-bed" type of letter writing to one that included personal observations and more selective reporting as a result of applying appropriate criteria. Criteria should remind students to be sincere, detailed and interested in the lives of the friends they are addressing.

Business Letters

Clear indications of purpose and required action are essential for business letters. If a business letter expresses bad news, the writer should begin the letter by focusing on purpose, develop the reasons for the bad news and conclude with a clear statement of the news. A business letter writer can also respond to an earlier request for action. In any event, self-assessment criteria will help to improve content and organization, as can be seen in the second letter shown in Chapter 1.

Film Reviews

In many parts of the world, school curricula are intensifying the emphasis on media study. If students are writing reviews of advertisements, magazine articles, television programs or films, they should employ specific criteria to revise the writing just as they would do for any other writing form.

Fortunately for teachers, references, periodicals, and teaching resources are becoming increasingly available. Such are useful in the development of self-assessment material. The following examples of criteria for film reviews were created by transforming information in media reference texts.

FILM REVIEWS: COMMON CRITERIA

- My review specifies the film genre, for example, western, romance, mystery, historical drama, modern drama, comedy, romance. ___ Yes ___ No
- Without revealing the outcome of the story, my review offers a brief overview of the setting, plot and major characters. ___ Yes ___ No
- My review indicates the film's audience appeal, in other words, who would enjoy it. ___ Yes ___ No
- My review indicates the filmmaker's intention, for example, to instruct, frighten, amuse. ___ Yes ___ No
- My review judges the extent to which the film meets its purpose by considering important aspects. For example:

    ___ If it sought to amuse, how was it amusing?

    ___ If it tried to frighten, how was it frightening?

    ___ If it portrayed challenge or conflict, was it convincing?

    ___ If it attempted to express ideas or lessons about life, were the themes important and effectively conveyed?

    ___ If the film emphasized symbolism, suspense or irony, how did it do so and how effective was its use of these techniques?

    ___ If the film focused on characters, were the characters convincingly developed through their actions, words and thoughts? What was revealed about them?

    ___ If the film was a drama, was the plot believable? Why?

    ___ If the film was a drama, were all the events included for an important purpose or reason? ___ Yes ___ No

---

- My review assesses the extent to which actors convincingly portrayed characters and met the challenges of their roles. ___ Yes ___ No. An example is ...
- My review comments on obvious technical strengths or faults, such as use of color, light, camera shots, special effects, sets, costumes and editing. ___ Yes ___ No
- My review attempts to relate comments to the experiences of readers by ...
- My writing most conveys a confident, authoritative tone in the following section: ...
-

Applying selected criteria immediately after viewing a film enabled one Grade 11 student to get out of the "summary trap." Prior to assessing her reviews, she provided plot summaries without commentary about artistic and technical qualities. Working with criteria while the film was fresh in her mind allowed her to venture into commentary.

Expository Writing

Expository writing seeks to inform the reader. To do so effectively, students should focus their writing on a specific topic and present relevant and well-organized reasons, evidence, illustrations and examples. Effective expository writing is sensitive to the audience in its selection of language and examples that the reader will understand.

EXPOSITORY WRITING: COMMON CRITERIA

- My topic is ...
- My specific purpose in writing about the topic is to ...
- My topic and purpose are clearly indicated to the reader. ___ Yes ___ No
- My introduction creates interest by ...
- My introduction offers a clear indication of the topic, purpose and contents of the writing. ___ Yes ___ No
- Every section of my writing is clearly focused on my topic and purpose. ___ Yes ___ No
- My writing attempts to relate explanations to the experiences and background of my readers by ...
- My writing develops main ideas directly related to my topic and purpose. The main ideas are as follows: ...

- I have checked that each of my main ideas is supported by examples, reasons, facts, illustrations or details. ___ Yes ___ No
- The paragraph or section that has the *most* complete and purposeful details begins with the sentence "..."
- My most imaginative or unusual support for a main idea is ...
- I have checked that words selected are specific and familiar to my audience. ___ Yes ___ No
- My conclusion is effective because it ...
- Each section of the writing is connected to the next because I have ...
- My writing best conveys a confident, authoritative tone in the following section: ...
-

One Grade 10 student who wrote shapeless expository text innovatively worked with both a checklist and color coding. To check that a draft offered the reader a preview in the introduction and subsequent paragraphs focused on the main topic, she highlighted main points in the introduction with different colors and points in following paragraphs with corresponding colors. The technique helped the student apply criteria related to organization more productively.

Persuasive Writing

Persuasive writing, a first cousin of expository writing, shares many features with exposition: the needs to identify a topic and purpose, to include evidence related to the topic and purpose, to consider language and examples that are appropriate to one's audience, to connect the writing sections, and to introduce and to conclude the piece. The difference between the two forms is that persuasive writing, such as an editorial or fund-raising letter, seeks to convince the reader to accept a belief or to take a specific course of action. To be successful, such writing demands specific evidence — it must be free of sweeping generalizations. Reading and analysing effective examples will help students to improve the presentation of evidence.

PERSUASIVE WRITING: COMMON CRITERIA

- My topic is ...
- My position on the topic is ...
- My topic and position are clearly indicated to the reader.
  ___ Yes ___ No
- Every section of my writing is clearly focused on my topic and purpose.
  ___ Yes ___ No
- My writing attempts to relate arguments and evidence to the experiences and backgrounds of my audience by ...
- My introduction creates interest by ...
- My introduction offers a clear indication of the topic, purpose, and content of my writing. ___ Yes ___ No
- The paragraph or section that *most* explicitly challenges an opposing position begins with the sentence "..."
- Each section of the writing is connected to the next because I have ...
- My writing best conveys a confident, authoritative tone in the following section ...
- My writing develops main ideas related to my topic and position. The main ideas are ...
- I have checked that each of my main ideas is supported by examples, reasons, facts, illustrations or details. ___ Yes ___ No
- The paragraph or section that has the *most* complete and purposeful evidence begins with the sentence "..."
- I have directly challenged opposing points of view. ___ Yes ___ No
- My conclusion is effective because ...
-

Dynamic Criteria Choices

Rarely will students deal only with criteria specific to a given writing form or purpose. More general criteria such as those outlined in Chapter 3 are bound to require their consideration too. As argued earlier, students should focus on five to ten criteria per assignment, criteria appropriate to critical writing variables and to their personal writing goals. In doing this, teachers and students will discover that few ready-made criteria forms are appropriate for their use. That is why this chapter concentrates on simply identifying a range of criteria for consideration.

5. Placing Student Assessment of Writing in the Context of Other Forms of Assessment

Student Assessment, Peer-Editing and Portfolios

Teachers often ask whether student assessment of writing is the same as peer-editing or as writing portfolios. It can be, but educators make a serious mistake when they use these terms synonymously. Peer-editing, writing portfolios, and self-assessment of student writing are all types of student assessment of writing.

Peer-editing, or peer-revision, has different meanings in professional literature. Sometimes, the term means rather unstructured discussion among students with questions such as "Tell me what you like about my writing ... Do you have any questions about my writing? ... Do you have any suggestions to help me improve my writing?" It becomes more powerful when it moves beyond rather general questions to more specific questions, such as "Help me locate tired words that could be more precise and colorful ... Which sentences could be combined to add interest to my composition?" However, peer-editing is still but one variation of student assessment of writing, always most effective when criteria are specific rather than general.

Portfolios represent another variation of student assessment of writing. Professional sources, including *Portfolio Assessment in the Reading-Writing Classroom* by Robert J. Tierney and others and *Student-Led Conferences* by Janet Millar Grant and colleagues, stress that portfolios are not merely collections of student work; the essence of the portfolio is *selection* rather than *collection*. In selecting writing for their portfolios, students apply specific criteria and thereby develop their writing ability.

Portfolios typically feature written comments by writers about why they have selected the pieces, what features do the pieces show and what their future goals as writers are. In completing this form of self-assessment, students benefit from knowledge of the language to describe specific features and an ability to recognize these features in their work.

Therefore, for many students, self-assessment practice with individual compositions, as discussed throughout this book, is a sensible entrée to a portfolio approach. In applying specific criteria to revise individual compositions, students learn the necessary language of assessment and learn to recognize features that their work possesses to analyse a collection of writing.

Clearly, students should engage in self-assessment of writing even if they are not assembling a portfolio. Beginning teachers are advised to foster self-assessment of individual compositions before introducing the more demanding task of developing a portfolio.

In summary, student self-assessment of writing can take different forms — individual revision with specific criteria, peer-revision with specific criteria and portfolios with evaluative comments based on familiarity with specific criteria.

Student Assessment of Writing and Performance Assessment

Although this book focuses on the self-assessment of writing, its suggested approach applies to all forms of performance assessment.

Performance assessment calls for the application of criteria to judge an activity or product which cannot be predicted beforehand. Examples are acting on the stage, composing and playing music, playing sports, solving problems and doing research reports. *Marking Success*, by Neil Graham and Jerry George, presents a valuable collection of performance assessment forms for reading, writing, listening and speaking that you may find useful.

Prespecified-response assessment, where the preferred answer is predetermined, contrasts with performance assessment. Familiar examples of prespecified response include true/false items, fill-in-the-blank, multiple choice tests and short answer questions. These techniques cannot be used to assess a performance.

Performance assessment, appropriate for much that is currently valued in education, readily applies to writing. Composing always results in writing different from any other writing; any given composition is somewhat unpredictable in specific content and technique. Writing *is* a performance.

Just as students learn through using specific criteria to revise writing, they benefit when they apply specific criteria to improve other performances as well. In recent years, teachers in art, music, and drama have increasingly engaged students in self-assessment activities. The same trend is noticeable in problem-solving approaches in mathematics. In many cases, teachers encourage students to write specific comments about their work in response to relevant criteria. This approach parallels student self-assessment of writing.

6. A Final Word

This book began with questions about those instructional strategies which most powerfully foster the development of student writing ability. The experience of teachers in the Calgary Catholic School District and the student work featured in this book argue that student self-assessment of writing with specific criteria is so critical that it should be a hallmark of a school's writing program. Therefore, when a school articulates important programming features, educators would be wise to include a statement about student self-assessment of writing. With confidence, teachers in a school should declare, as have many teachers from the Calgary Catholic School District:

> *In our school,*
> *we encourage students*
> *to employ specific criteria*
> *to revise their writing*
> *in all grades and all subjects.*
> *In our school,*
> *we do not assess writing*
> *until students have assessed it first.*
> *In our school,*
> *we always seek to use assessment*
> *to help students*
> *set personal goals and*
> *develop their confidence*
> *and ability as writers.*

With such a policy, a school can do much to answer parents' and students' questions about how to promote stronger student writing.

Recommended References

Student Resources

Barry, James. *Language to Go*. Scarborough, ON: Nelson Canada, 1994.

This student reference includes exercises designed to improve conventional usage in writing. Its most attractive feature is the editing checklist approach for matters of usage.

Iveson, Margaret, and Samuel Robinson. *Language Arts Survival Guide*. Scarborough, ON: Prentice-Hall, 1993.

This student reference includes helpful information about a variety of writing forms and about helpful revision strategies. In addition, the book features hundreds of suggestions for effective reading, writing, speaking, listening and viewing.

Scott, Ruth. *The Student Editor's Guide to Words*. Scarborough, ON: Gage, 1991.

Scott's valuable reference reminds students of strategies and patterns for spelling and word usage. It is intended to be used as an editing tool.

Selected Professional Resources

Aker, Don. *Hitting the Mark: Assessment Tools for Teachers*. Markham, ON: Pembroke, 1995.

Aker's comprehensive consideration of assessment and evaluation practice emphasizes clear articulation of expectations and student self-assessment.

Glatthorn, Allan A. *Writing in the Schools, Improvement Through Effective Leadership*. Ann Arbor, MI: Books on Demand (originally published by NAASP, 1981).

Glatthorn outlines research-supported practice related to instruction in writing. His presentation of strategies, followed by a look at successful and unsuccessful writers, is particularly useful.

Graham, Neil, and Jerry George. *Marking Success*. Markham, ON: Pembroke, 1992.

Graham and George present a valuable collection of performance evaluation forms. Their emphases on self-assessment and goal setting are consistent with the focus of this book.

Grant, Janet Millar, Barbara Heffler, and Kadri Mereweather. *Student-Led Conferences: Using Portfolios to Share Learning with Parents*. Markham, ON: Pembroke, 1995.

In their advice about student-led conferences, the authors underline the importance of student ownership of assessment and goal setting.

Hansen, Jane. *When Writers Read*. Portsmouth, NH: Heinemann, 1987.

Hansen offers practical advice focused on the importance of "reading like a writer" and on fostering student ownership of self-assessment.

Hillocks, George, Jr. *Research on Written Composition, New Directions for Teaching*. Urbana, IL: National Council of Teachers of English, 1986.

Hillocks' summary of research on written composition challenges much current practice while powerfully supporting student self-assessment of writing.

Moffett, James, and Betty Jane Wagner. *Student-Centered Language Arts, K-12: A Handbook for Teachers*. 4th Edition. Portsmouth, NH: Boynton-Cook, 1990.

This handbook is a valuable reference for teachers who believe that students develop language ability through active involvement in personally significant contexts.

Tierney, Robert J. et al. *Portfolio Assessment in the Reading-Writing Classroom*. Norwood, MA: Christopher-Gordon Publishers, 1991.

Tierney's text stresses the importance of student self-assessment and ownership of reading and writing portfolios.

Weaver, Constance. *Grammar for Teachers Perspectives and Definitions*. Urbana, IL: National Council of Teachers of English, 1979.
    In reviewing years of research on the applicability of grammatical terminology to reading and writing ability, Weaver argues for instruction in the meaningful context, something that is consistent with the approach to student-self assessment recommended in this book.

Zemelman, Steven, and Harvey Daniels. *A Community of Writers: Teaching Writing in the Junior and Senior High School*. Portsmouth, NH: Heinemann, 1988.
    In their comprehensive review of writing process approaches, Zemelman and Daniels usefully emphasize Hillocks' summary of research.

Computer Programs

Writer's Workbench 5.O., E.M.O. Educational Software, 1250 Shore Road, Napierville, IL 60563.
    Intended to complement classroom instruction, this computer system helps students revise with specific criteria and in response to feedback furnished by the program.

Index

Blackline Masters

Here, for teachers' convenience, are a number of resources that appear in some form within the text proper. They may be photocopied or adapted as required to meet your needs in the classroom.

SELF-ASSESSMENT OF WRITING

Name: _____ Date: _____ Title: _____

I. PURPOSE, AUDIENCE, FORM:

In the attached piece, my purpose is to _____

_____

my audience is _____

the writing form is _____

II. SPECIFIC CRITERIA:

The following criteria are important to the attached piece of writing.

CRITERION: _____

_____

My Self-Assessment/Revisions:

CRITERION: _____

_____

My Self-Assessment/Revisions:

CRITERION: _____

_____

My Self-Assessment/Revisions:

SELF-ASSESSMENT OF GOALS IN WRITING

Name: _____

Grade: _____ Date: _____

      From: _____ To: _____

             Date   Date

GOALS ACHIEVED   GOALS STILL TO BE ACHIEVED

ASSESSMENT FORM FOR WRITING

Name: _____ Date: _____

For each criterion listed, students and teachers rate the composition by writing the score and their initials in the appropriate box beside each criterion. Peers who assess the composition should also include their initials with the rating in the appropriate box.

CRITERIA	VERY EVIDENT	SOMEWHAT EVIDENT	NOT EVIDENT
	6 5	4 3	2 1 0

EVALUATION OF STRENGTHS/ GOALS ACHIEVED		SUGGESTIONS FOR LEARNING AND FOR REVISION	
STUDENT	TEACHER	STUDENT	TEACHER

THINKING ABOUT MY WRITING PROCESS

Name: _____

	Record Assignment Number *Beside Strategies Used*	*My Goals as a Writer*

PREWRITING
Drawing/Diagramming
Observing
Listening to Reader
Listening to Speaker
Brainstorming
Reading for Information
Role Playing
Interviewing
Questioning
Sharing in Small Groups
Contributing to Discussion
Viewing Activities
Writing to Explore
Note-Making
Story Boarding

REVISING
Reading Work Aloud
Listening to Work Read
Conferring with Teacher
Peer-Editing
Individual Revision
Individual Proofreading

SHARING
Taping of Writing
Displaying of Writing
Reading Final Drafts
Publishing Writing
Dramatized Writing
Putting Writing to Use
Other Sharing

SMALL-GROUP WORK STUDENT ASSESSMENT FORM

Criteria   *My Goals for Small-Group Work*

_____ 1. I helped the group review its
          task.

_____ 2. I contributed relevant ideas;
          I stayed on topic.

_____ 3. I listened carefully to other
          group members.

_____ 4. I was open-minded about
          different interpretations or
          understandings.

_____ 5. I helped the group stay
          focused on its task.

_____ 6. I contributed to the summary
          which concluded the group
          work.

_____ 7. I encouraged all members of
          the group to contribute.

COMMON CONTENT AND ORGANIZATION CRITERIA

- The purpose of my writing is to ...

- I have checked that all parts of my writing relate directly to my purpose. ___ Yes ___ No

- I have checked that all of my main ideas are supported with examples, reasons, facts, illustrations or details. ___ Yes ___ No

- The paragraph or section that has the most complete and purposeful details begins with the sentence: ...

- The most imaginative or unusual section related to my purpose is ...

- The part of my writing which best demonstrates that I care about my purpose and topic is ...

- My opening creates interest by ...

- The writing closes effectively by ...

- I effectively employ transitions in the following places: ...

- The main points or sections of my writing have been arranged in the following order: ...

- I have checked that the order of my main points or sections is clear for my reader. ___ Yes ___ No

- The part of my writing that best conveys the sense that no other writer could have written it is ...

- I have checked that my writing follows expectations for its form (e.g., business letter, short story, résumé). ___ Yes ___ No

-

COMMON SEMANTIC AND SYNTACTIC CRITERIA

- I have checked that all of my words are precise.
  ___ Yes ___ No

- Three particularly precise words are _____, _____, and _____.

- A particularly effective or colorful expression is ...

- I have varied my sentence lengths and beginnings.
  ___ Yes ___ No

- An effective longer sentence is ...

- An effective short sentence is ...

- I have checked that all of my sentences are complete.
  ___ Yes ___ No

- I have checked that sentences are correctly ended with a period, question mark, exclamation point, or with a semi-colon between two connected, complete thoughts.
  ___ Yes ___ No

-